LOST IN YOU

SOUL CONNECTION

BHUMIKA TEWARI

TO MY MOTHER

Couldn't have done it without your support and mental health issues made
all of it possible.

Contents

Contents

Contents

Contents

Preface

In today's fast paced world, mankind is too busy to earn a lively hood even at the cost of individual happiness and the poems I have written in this book sometimes questions this society and asks the readers to tarry a bit and search for their individual happiness. I have also included poems based on various individual thoughts to the questions that life asks us. These thoughts can also be referred as the unspoken words which without a listener would erode the mind from within. All my poems are a mirror to the real world of the 21st century and I hope that readers will find them relatable. I have written these poems based on various human emotions and supressed desires representing the state of mind in various situations. I hope that my readers will enjoy my piece of work.

Acknowledgements

Hi all,

I can't possibly thank everyone who has contributed to this book.

Everyone who ever came to my life has played a part. You all know who you are, so in case I missed you out, like always -------- sorry.

This book would not have been possible without the generous support of my family members, friends and well wishers. Thank you all being a part of my life.

The ones I would like to thank here are :

God, for giving me so much.

Tam particularly grateful to my publication house,

Poetries club Publication especially **Utkarsh Sir** for his immense contribution to publish this book. I appreciate for their constant support of all my efforts.

The editors at Poetries Club Publication, for their relentless attempts to make the book better.

My critics, For helping me improve and keeping my ego down.

Special thanks to my parents, **Mrs Kaberi Tewari** and **Mr Avijit Tewari** for their support, love and sacrifice during the writing of this book. Special thanks to my Sir and my bestie Jancy for encouraging me to complete this book. I affectionately dedicate this book to them.

Finally, thank you readers, you are the best judge and my source of inspiration. Any suggestions and constructive criticism by the readers for improvements of this book will highly be appreciated.

About The Book

Spoken straight from the heart, these poems can only be classified under the umbrella of emotions of life and hope. Unbounded by any serious topic, **Lost In You** book after my two books Rapid Rafts and Sort of Lost , explores life and it's facets. These poems are more than lines and words describing feelings, they are a reflection of humanity, life and the experiences that connect us all, reminding us that we are here, right now. The thoughts are managed to be put into words, giving unnameable feelings, names, emotions to lines and life to poems. The poems in the book are mostly romantic, nature lovers and at the same time sad, miserable also but can be laughed upon too with a less attention to that. No matter how much you relate to one of them, know that Poetry in itself more is music to eyes and it always meant to be felt and forgotten. Rest love has always been tragic and mostly meaningless and tragic.

1. My Love

Days have past & years have passed,

My love for you will always last…

We have a strong bonding of love, though with fights & tears,

But as now we are together, there are no more fears…

I am your heart & you are my heartbeat,

There will never be anyone for our love to compete…

In the new beginning of our life; with me & you beside,

I will always need you by my side….

There may be lots of problems that may arise,

But together we will fight & once again rise….

Always be with me as you are my only support ever,

And that I will need you now & forever….

We have a long way to go together,

And if you are with me, there is nothing to bother….

No matter what hardships we might need to go thru,

I promise I will now & forever be with you….

All I want is to tell this to you,

That I will always need you & I will always love you.

2. Empty Promises

Truth knocks at the door at ultimate times
And it strikes me harder time and again;
I promised to love, the almighty weapon
Of human's emotions and unknown feelings.
It was this day that year, you promised me
That I will be your only one as you are to me;
I kept my end which was a waste of time
As you on the other end never held the rope.
It was not a single promise from my side,
But a collective vows of every inch of me;
My eyes promised it'd not look anyone else
And as did my heart to never build walls.
Even though many have said you were faking,
And that you're using me only for pleasure;
My ears as promised never told my brain,
And brain never grew such doubts about you.
But how much ever we conceal everything,
Your faces came out, one by one after an year;
Your promises were hollow just like your heart,
The truth knocked me out gaining its throne.

3. My Heart Still Finds You..

My heart still finds you
In the valleys of the flowers,
In the waves of the ocean,
And in the corner of my heart
My heart still finds you .
Sun rising to sun dawning
In the middle of the sky,
In the vastness of the space,
My heart still finds you…
In the night when world Is asleep,
I write you on the crumpled white paper.
I bleed you on the vessels of the flowers,
This way my heart still finds you…
From missing you to loving you
My eternal love still reminds you .
In the aroma of this Romance,
My heart still finds you….

4. The Unsung Song

They say I am full of life
I'm filled with song and dance
I live life to the hilt
I miss no rapturous chance
I don't believe in crying
I'm jubilant and strong
There are courageous people
I've been with them for long.
Now I have a dark secret
I have fallen in love
It made me docile, fey and
Very delicate like a dove
I'm not street smart
I've dreams in my eyes
Love gave me wings of fancy
I'd soar high up the skies
But nothing lasts forever.
One day I lost my beau
I do not know the reason
Why must he leave me and go
My vivacity is no more
Gone is my gleeful laughter
I feel I have to close
My life's happiest chapter

Would he ever see in my eyes
Un-spilled drop of a tear
Would he, again, my unsung song
With its injured melody, hear.

5. The Lost Love

I loved her for many years;
I lost her love when we were apart;
She changed her mind for many fears
For my poor life, she threw her heart
To another guy who does not care
In her love, he is too proud
Of himself, and does she dare
To be his darling even he is coward;
Oh my love! Why did you change
From purity to such a state
Of impurity, you are so strange;
Your life is hard and your fate
To be alone all of the time;
To be alive in the rhyme.

6. An Ode on Forgiveness

I forgive you
For all the hopes and dreams.
I forgive you
All the broken promises we made.
I forgive you for not being my anchor
When I was being lapped up by the tides
I forgive you for not lighting my way when I was all alone and stumbling
through Arden.
I forgive you for our imaginary baby boy
Who has your grey eyes and my curls.
I forgive you for painting the woody cottage down the hill.
I forgive you for sprouting saps of tenacity and desire.
I forgive you for reading me Jane Eyre.
I forgive you for making me fall in love with black coffee.
I forgive you for teaching me all about bitcoins, NFT and International
relations.
I forgive you for teaching me how to play für elise.
I forgive you for making me laugh to the point I cried.
I forgive you for teaching me how to bake.
I forgive you for all the late night rides through the busy streets,
*The smell on Pani puris**
I can still taste it on my tongue.
I forgive you for making my parents laugh.
I forgive you for making my dog fall in love with you.

I forgive you for giving hope to your mother, I met her at the store last week
She still calls me on my birthdays.
I forgive you for connecting me with your father
Did you know he is sober for three years?
Has a six-year-old terrier
We still goes for a fishing day.
I forgive you for all the matches that you missed of your buddies from school.
Last month I saw T_ and had a coffee with him.
I forgive you for not stepping up when little Emma got cheated on.
She has a baby boy, just like ours.
She even named him after you.
I forgive you for all the missed football matches
I forgive you for making Bruno Mars not feel the same without you.
I forgive you for being in my heart after all these years
Not allowing me to completely move on.
I forgive you for your nasty drinking
I forgive you for not being here with me while watching Grey's Anatomy.
I forgive you for getting into that car after I was on my knees begging you to stop.
I forgive you for making me fall in love, promising me eternity.
And I finally forgive you for living this world behind
Hope you have found the closure that you were searching for these twenty years.

7. Relationships

Relationships die faster than
Leaves upon the trees
The bunch scatters rapidly
When goodwill snaps the ties
True, no one person matches the other
In views they do divide
Unwanted thoughts scatter the vision
When clouds thicken the tide
Too many individuals soon grow tall
With independent views
That clash and collide
Like tidal waves upon the growling sea
No one sees eye to eye
The gap is far and wide
Egos live on and divide
Until submerged by the tide
The 'I' is strong the relationship puny
When 'they' decide to drive
Your wheels and hang you by 'their' side
Their will is strong they drag you by it
Mum is the answer you know
For if you resent, the gap tears wider
No strings remain to bind
The knots harsh grown

LOST IN YOU

The feelings die untold
No 'meds' can heal the wounds gutted deep
Icicles hang … so…co..l..d.
Some have the will to shoot and win
The gun on another's shoulders wide
The trigger pulls the shot is shot
A lonesome way it goes
Somewhere lost in pain and bruises
Submerged too deep to hide
The split is driven torn unhealed
Bleeding, oozing to the core
Silent tears roll down to hide
The broken wings it bore.

8. I Owe You

To the Sun, I owe you
For the warmth and happiness.
Every shine sweeps the entire space
And reign the day as bright as the Sun itself.
To the Moon, I owe you
For the peace of time and a joyful night.
Silent but with much brilliance,
The nights are awoken to a melodious music.
To nature, I owe you
For the beauty and diversity of life.
Evergreen and serene,
The harmony in exposition is an art of a creator.
To the leaders, I owe you
For guidance, inspiration, and wisdom.
Selfless and devoted service toward humanity,
Truly defining the call of Godly actions.
To the parents, I owe you
For all the love, care, and nurturing of me.
The unconditional and unique bond is affirmed,
I pay respect and gratitude for everything.
To all my friends, I owe you
For maintaining a good relationship and rendering unconditional
support.
Friendships are of varying colour

But true friends are rare and precious.
To the world, I owe you
For the lovely home, you've created.
No one is deprived of such privileges
As the law of coexistence is at its best exhibit.
To my sweetheart, I owe you
For the trust, love, and faith in me.
You are heavenly gifted to me and my family,
You are the Northstar and the torch bearer of a future.

9. Relationship

We were not related by blood
We had a special bond
I looked at him shyly with love
All he did was to respond.
The chemistry was working
Developing into romance
We tied the knot and formed a new
Relationship by design and chance.
But the food of love is despair
And sorrow of separation,
Familiarity breeds contempt
Proximity diminishes passion.
So, our alliance took a dip
His family did not like me
It was insulted, ridiculed and
With harsh words spiked me.
Instead of standing by me
He succumbed to family pressure
I simply quit with a new wisdom
That blood is thicker than water.
Now, I don't form relationships
I don't give love any tag or name
If my feelings are real and deep
I think I've attained my aim.

10. Love Untold…

She gazed at him, intently
Knowing he was no ordinary child
He was fast asleep in his cradle
Swaddled, in a snowy flannel.
Her eyes were neither wet nor moist,
As she held him to her bosom.
He smelt of freshly baked bread,
As a mild smell of incense
Wafted in the air.
He was fine and healthy
And breathing swiftly
She held him, nearer, to her lips
And gently
Whispered into his tiny ears: 'Aditya'
He trembled and let out a shriek
As she stood adoring him
With a pride
Only, a mother possess.
She clothed him,
Fed him,
And spun sleepless nights
And restless days
Into bright and cheerful ones.
She was and still is-

His light and shadow.
As years passed by
The little one outgrew his mother
Yet, she holds him to her bosom
Knowing he is an extraordinary child.

11. A Platonic Love

I know you are always mine,
And so my heart ponders to dine,
With your cheerfully and benign
Because my love for you is divine.
Do you remember the day we met?
The charming eyes I can never forget.
You were with your buddies and a booklet
Staring at your beloved Juliet.
Recall the times I was there to console
Climbing stairs to meet my soul
My throat was dry, hands in tremble,
Like a prisoner, on parole.
The love I bestowed on you was insane
Looking at you from the windowpane
Your smile was driving me crazy again
Take a trip down Memory lane.
We shared our times in platonic love,
That was heavenly high above
Hoping to cherish you one day
Because we have a thousand memories on our way.

12. Incarnation of Love!

13. Love And Love Will Meet In Us

Love and Love will meet in us,
Love and Love coming from the heart.
Love and Love will meet in us
When we come together to endure and to last.
The love it is of you and me
That's leadin' on the way of enduring peace,
Keepin' away the shadows that want to mislead,
Givin' the warmth and hope of the free.
Listen, baby, it is easy to see:
Fortunate you are if you have found the key,
The key to your heart that makes you real,
The key to our hearts that bring the real,
A life of true being and unity,
A life of happy harmony,
A life of conscious being together,
A life of growth into the better.

14. First Love or Life

The hubby said to his spouse,
"Which is first, love or life?"
His spouse heartily replied –
The love from where the life begins
The water flows
The rose blooms
The earth grows
The sky spreads beyond our imagination.
The hubby thought for a moment
Then, he makes the meanings
When love exists
Water assists rose to bloom
Rose makes the earth beautiful
Then the earth becomes meaningful
When it has the vast sky of full freedom.
Love begins from hearts-
From natural hearts
When life begins from heartless brain
It bears and pairs numerous pain
Thus, let's bring up life from love
As love is whole and life a part
Remember!
Life is seen as a knife at present
Which cuts the pipe

Through which lived-love goes on
Where it has to go.
When the love ends, it becomes a pole
When the life ends, it becomes a black hole.

15. Recall of Love

Recall of love, a memory so sweet,
A feeling that still dances in my feet.
It brings a smile, a warmth in my heart,
A love that still sets me apart.
It was a time, a special moment in life,
When two hearts beat, in perfect rhythm and rhyme.
When laughter filled the air and love was new,
And all the world was painted in shades of blue.
But time goes by, and life moves on,
And memories fade, like a gentle dawn.
Yet the recall of love, it lingers still,
A reminder of a time, when life was thrill.
So I hold on tight, to this memory of love,
For it's a treasure, sent from heaven above.
It's a precious gift, that I'll always keep,
And the recall of love, will always be, a beautiful memory.

16. Symbol Of Love

In the long lost ages of time.

In the crux of the eternal and divine.

There are stories we hear that has given humans faith and belief to

incline.

In between the creation and destruction there has always been you two on

the path to

procreation.

What is start and what is beyond?

What is present and what is gone?

Names sages have never forgotten for long, and always depended on their

power of creation

and form.

They say they know you ,still there are who lost all eternity to know you.

They say you are kind and at the same time have the utmost power to

create this universe and

be divine .

There is beautiful tale of two entities so refine.

It difficult to put words to understand them and define.

A folklore so beautiful which never ceases to fail, a

companionship which many crave to gain.

The blend call Shiv & Shakti,the most powerful love the eras have seen.

There are lessons in your love that makes me wonder in my heart and

lean.

Love can conquer all and be benign.

You can come from different backgrounds and still be fine.
You can hold hands and leave the comforts behind.
You can be equal and still be individual.
You can have rights over each other but not control.
You can have devotion, without matter of insecurity notion.
You can learn from each other,
Work together and still be one.
You can have each other's back
And team up to solve problems to make them undone.
You experience pain together that's a part of life,
But if soul meets it's twin flame you are happily done for life.
You can be powerful &
Calm yet fight for your family and loved ones .
You should be beyond, time, ages ,people, problems, kids, universe nothing
should be able to
break you apart.
You taught as partners one should always speak their mind, one's
suggestion are always to be
listened and never to be undermined.
Words are less ,the knowledge is negligible no matter how I want to
describe.
My heart lingers to find a love and a soul to vibe.
I can only say that this bond is far and beyond anyone to fathom.
We can only try and crave to have such a companionship attention.
If one can't have it all then at least experience a fraction.
An epitome tale that makes you wonder, that love is your right but you
have to surrender.

17. Come Back

Come back the way you was,
Suddenly without you everything seems pause,
Remember the time when we met,
The awkwardness and our first date,
The genuine smiles that were spread across,
I remember the way you used to eat sauce,
It was your heart that melted me in your warmth,
I was so free with you, no protocols, no norms ,
We together builded everything from a single peck,
I miss you and your kisses on my neck,
It was like a dreamland we formed,
Just never realised how everything just vanished in a weird storm,
But still we have to stand again,
Firm and strong, we need to build our den,
Come back the way you were,
Realise how it all just happened and the cause,
See where you went wrong,
How can we stop singing our life songs,
Gather all the strength again,
Don't fall in vain,
I am there, right there where we first met,
Waiting for you to come back and lets start great.

18. Feelings

A thing which comes unknown,
Whether it's sorrow or love at most,
Excitement or fright may be these are just words,
But these express the inner feelings of our heart.
Sometimes we deny the fact that feelings take, the most space in our
hearts,
Even when it's true we are scared to admit that,
Emotions make you weak and broken inside,
It means a lot to our heartheart.

19. Leman

The rosy ribbon might not forever be secured around my wrist,
His sheeny eyes forever will not dwell on me,
My subdued smile no longer will heal his ruthless agony,
Our giggles forever might disappear in the daze of despair,
No longer might the heart shaped chocolate be for him and me but,
Will he grant a part of his heart to me?
Tangled is that band still in our souls,
Never will it either away from our blossom of trust,
His love is what keeps me entangled to him, His words
When I sway on slumber is like lullaby to ears,
He is an universal diamond creature to me,
Will he grant a part of his heart to me?
Researches I did a lot to find the true meaning of love,
Never did anyone tell me that it was him,
Still now I don't know what it is,
Maybe we find lemans in dreams and desires,
In real he is a healer and my safekeeper,
Will he grant a part of his heart to me?

20. Harlequin

Lately I haven't been in love,
The prospect scares me, or the lack thereof,
I haven't adored anything,
The closet I have gotten to redeeming myself is looking at wild flowers
And suffocating myself with the desire to crush them with my bare feet
And to baptize myself with their ever drying blood;
Last week I saw a blossoming home,
My heart groaned in all it's stillness,
I felt the familiar slither in my blood, the overwhelming necessity to
Watch flames curl around their doomed fates,
Around noon the dissonance inside me births unprecedented chaos;
My insides burn when I allow my conscious to wreak havoc on myself,
There is a darkness that roams somewhere in my ribs,
I've screamed my throat raw and my clothes are stained from all the
Blood I've coughed up,
My insides flood a dark thick stream these days,
I tell myself that it's okay to let the darkness bleed out at times;
Soon I realize that I'm not convincing anyone.

21. Feelings Within

They said its time to move on Move on from far apar Forgetting the
unforgetful
But its easier than done
She with a numb face replied saying okay….
But deep down within the struggles with her feelings within
The feelings within
As she walked through the lane
She thought how easy it was for some to hurt people…
How easy to ignore her when she need their company
She questioned herself about being unloved
The feelings Within
As she felt when the one gave her the worst of the wounds
Who mocked her for being cribby
It was non another than the one she trusted……..
Talked with her for hours…
She realized how she was trusting people too easily
Not realizing the world is brutal
As brutal as sharpness of the knife Which shatters the people…
As she walked through the Lane
She decided to move on Cover her emotions with a mask
A mask of smile
A mask which could hide her emotions…
Emotions of dejection
The feelings that would remain hidden in a mask forever….

The feelings that would remain hidden in a mask forever…

• 29 •

22. Every Inches Of My Skin

On my every inches of my skin,
Your essence always win, Every touch traumatize my body,
Your hotness control my mood,
From rude to Hornier, your touch swings me…. DUDE From innocence
to dirtier,
In clothes and then nude, Every inch is yours,
If you'll adore
Like sweet baby or doll,
Never try to treat me like a whore,
You'll make your image fall,
Every inch of my skin
Is thirsty for the same sin pleasure with sensuality.

23. Hidden Heart

24. Darling To You

Dazzling to the soul,
Unique to the heart,
Anger to the brain,
Rustler as rain,
Rational from the vein,
You're like an orphean smell,
Queen of a garden,
Hardest from the mind,
Blend your troubles in the sand
Let joy sprout in your land,
Don't get away from my hand,
Honour to me grand,
Getting you in my band,
O my precious almond,
May your life shine like a diamond.

25. One Last Walk

I wish someday
We could walk miles
Down Street
Towards the Sunset,
I would hold your hand,
And look into your eyes
If I say I'm not crying
Don't trust my lies.
I would hold you in my arms
As evening turns night
You'd lean on my shoulder
Locking our fingers tight,
If you'd go tired
I'd take you to home
Hold you for the entire night
Scared of being alone.

26. Never Apart

27. Life of Lilies

28. You Are The Universe

Inside a dark room You stood in front of mirror,
A cloth filled with self doubt tied around your eyes,
Guilt stuck to Skin,
Fear was waiting for your demise.
With every breath I saw you Break,
Into million pieces of Opaque,
Trying to hide all Your Struggles,
Finding Light in your miseries.
The pieces of your most cherished memories,
Starting piercing through armour of guilt,
Tearing the cloth of self doubt,
You stared at the Mirror mesmerized by the sight.
In front of mirror you stood like work of Actions,
Accepting Yourself from the Heart,
A divine being made up galaxy,
It was a beautiful sight to view.
The mirror reflected your inner light,
The dark room became bright,
Your light spread across the World,
You Are The Universe!!

29. Hidden Feelings

Hide, intension and fears behind smiles
Hide, heart of truth behind faces
Hide, beautiful smiles behind filters
Hide, true love amid fortress of insecurities
Hide, broken heart behind hurtful words
Hide, we are shadows in the dark,
Lost in the land of uncertainties,
With a roadmap of confusions,
Aimlessly wandering around,
Until we spot a speck of light,
Guiding our feet toward clear Skies.

30. You Are Verily Going to Shine

Sitting below the wide welkin we gaze

Don't you feel like it to chase

Peaks and valleys may come in your thruway

Day you bloom with the success that will surely display

Work incessantly, with peace

Face the case, with courage

Your problems will impulsively cease

Let your plight admire

How strong's your desire

To reach your goal

With whole and soul

Revere something divine,

You are verily going to shine.

31. Tapestry of Petals

Grew up into a magnificent being
Each with its own shape and size
Forming a bundle of joy and peace
The gleaming petals radiated light
The bunch ate the lunch together
Healthily satisfied within themselves
Strong companionship with each other
Celebrating with the rains and winds like Elves
Weather did wither them with age
Separating them from there paradise
Harmoniously living at every stage
Bidding a happy farewell on each others demise
The tapestry of the life of each petal
Spreads aroma by blossoming into a flower
Love is the only virtue on which they settle
Accepting and respecting each others powers.

32. Bring back Love

It doesn't feel like titanic anymore.
Please don't let Romeo and Juliet die.
Is this love story burning into ashes?
My feet aren't touching the stairs.
My gown won't read my poems.
The kiss didn't reach my lips.
The waves didn't scream my name.
Did my tears reach the blossom?
The candles are inhaling all the oxygen.
Rotten-smelling raindrops.
My blood is staining the floor.
Gold dripping down the wall.
I don't know how to speak.
I don't know what to hear.
All I know are the love story in the books.

33. Sleeping Beauty

Under the quilt of the thickest wool,
She smiles in the memory's pool,
She bites her lips to talk with me,
I get flooded in her sweetest sea.
She winks her eyes and steals my heart,
She looks like the iconic art,
Hidden behind the mascaric folds of eyes,
She is my one and only choice.
She looks like a teddy doll,
For whom I always fall,
Gazing at her bewitching eyes' balls,
She is my favorite voice of calls.
Hiding behind the thickness of blanket,
She looks like an art so perfect,
She wins my heart and drag me to her,
As smiles like a little star.
In the ocean of her sassy eyes,
I fall for her with no bias,
She is the sweetest song I ever heard,
For she is my poem and I am her bard.

34. Eucalyptus

Your eyes don't reflect the eucalyptus radiance
And I bare my forehead to the clouds passing by
And contemplate why
When I have grown the uncalled-for habit
Of comparing your existence to the eternal
Beauty of an irresolute thought
Vanished into the air in an imitation of the infantile leaves
As you make your way over to where I sit ramrod straight
Because your very appearance has me unmade.

35. Crying Onion

36. Why Disband The Two In Love

I once knew a boy, a prince, by his blood,
I'm etching his love story, being the lad of the king's courtly bard.
Outdid he many, even me, in adventures and hunts all along,
Our friendship dwelled, as wide as the Saharan belt, an army of two, yet
strong.
During the day, we would practice with bows and arrows,
And even though, the meagre meal, I ate in my humble abode,
Chirpy evenings, with horses and mares, drums and snares,
Would always surely follow.
One day, during a game, he witnessed a slender, rural dame,
Even though she tried to bury her amazement, he would never again be
the same.
In many ways, he tried, her heart to secure,
And, like a fairy, in the prairies, even her heart did follow.
Both, full of dreams, and hand in hand,
Verily, unnoticed their love did not.
But, their childish hearts, did beat as one,
Secretly, they married, this to me the prince had told.
I could not risk, foolhardy Temptation's snare to mar their union,
So, unnerved in my ways, I took to what his friend ought to have done,
I inked a letter to the king, to cement their ties for eons,
When he can disband armies, why disband the two in pristine love?

37. Closer

We are now in two places
Not in heaven, not in hell
But somewhere in the middle
Not together not distant
But somewhere near
Once we sat in heaven
In heavenly bliss, holding hands,
Thinking of the future, giggling
For our worst jokes.
In the beginning of separation
We never knew, we loved or
Cared for each other.
And in the end
Time taught us
The more distant we are
The closer we became.

38. Existence of You

Every time I look at the morning sky

I see your blue-almond eyes looking at mine

Through clouds far away from my land.

Every time I hear a cuckoo sing

I hear your voice, which never stopped singing Madhuvanti raga in my

ears.

Every time I touch the jasmines in my garden

I remember those days you secretly

Pinned your hair with the flowers

I kept it on your table.

Every time I walk through meadows

I embrace the grass that touched

The silver anklets on your feet.

Every time I stroll through saffron shops of the bazaar

I could smell your wet body

Entangled around mine

During the rainy nights we spent

Under the banyan tree.

You soon went away from me

Like a mystery that never got revealed

Leaving me alone in the darkness

You were afraid to be.

But I know you exist in me.

The atoms of love,

That you left in me, holds me together
In times of grief.
My love, your existence is an eternity.

· 47 ·

39. Looking for you

I don't want to write about you
But here I am
No reasons, no hopes
But here I am
Everyday, at midnights,
I don't care what is right, Looking for you
In empty dark rooms
Here I am
Telling people how much you loved
Watching them giving the sympathetic looks
I wonder, often
Why can't I be the one you choose
Telling myself its alright Loosing control every other night
I don't want to write about you
But here I am
Living you through the songs Kissing you through the memories
Here I am. Here I will ,
Stay Looking for you
In empty dark rooms.

40. Fear(Less) Forever

She stood in the dark alone,
The breeze was bleak and cold ,
She dreaded walking to comfort,
They called Home
Why?
She feared they would stalk her,
Her inner essence got disheartened.
But as she closed her eyes, she realised ,
The goddess she was!
She felt strong
Her blood carried passion She fights for her rights
To slay the darkness of their sight.
She was escorted to her right place with grace
With no fright to face.
She perceived that fear was futile
And no soul could ever dare to dim her smile.

41. Legacy of love

I, never, was inclined,
To earn extra wealth,
I loved art and culture,
And things about mental health.
I taught my children that,
Money has its own worth,
But there're more important things,
Under the sky and on the earth.
Knowledge, education, hard work,
Morals, empathy, and ethics,
Respect for all relationships,
Cleanliness and a sense of civics.
I will go from this world,
Empty-handed and alone,
No property I will leave,
For my kids when I'm gone.
Except for a legacy of love,
Plus the lessons I have taught,
Which are treasures of values, are,
More precious than money could've bought.

42. The Unsaid Love

I Never Should Have Said Goodbye,
But If You Really Liked Me
Why Would You Let Me Go
And If You Really Needed Me
Why Would You Turn Your Back On Me
If I Ever Saw You Someday
Would You Smile At Me?
Or Maybe You're With Someone Else,
I'll Just Be Glad Seeing You Happy!
I Wish Someday,
We will Sit By The Ocean
Making Fun Of How We Got Seperated
Laughing At Each Other,
Remembering How Complicated It Was
Hoping That You Wouldn't Let Go
Love Would Be A Bit Of A Word,
After all, That's All I Know.

43. The Most Beautiful Poem

The cuisine I had yesterday
Looked absolutely normal,
I wasn't impressed by its appearance.
But I was on cloud nine
When I tasted it and
The smell was savory too.
Sometimes the most beautiful poem
Might look normal
The words used may not
Sound lovely and wonderful.
But after tasting its words
You feel beautiful and satisfied.

44. Fading Away

That place was dark like hell
But there was a light that led my way
That light gave me happiness
It taught me how to be happy
How to enjoy life
How to overcome my fears
How to face people
But now I feel that,
The only light from there is fading away
It is fading day by day and I don't know,
When it will be dark
I'm doing whatever I can to protect that light
I don't want that light to fade
But if it is to fade then no one can stop it
It's going to fade away
It's fading away.

45. Cataclysmic Bleach

Lying on the meadows or on the cold floor,
She ceaselessly inquest in herself the shambles,
She speaks flawless with no rumbles,
She seems outstanding with shimmering dissembles.
Withered away is her cherishing hopes,
She nurtures neither desire nor dreams,
The world being a black and white TV,
She could visualize everything except the variety shades.
Her eyes are all confused covered with mist,
Her heart is numb like stones with torment,
She looks tough like rugged stones,
Rolling down and breaking into mere dust.

46. The Memories of Tomorrow

How could you forget the memories we made,
The kisses we shared and the foundation we laid,
When all I can think about is the love I adored,
And the times I gave you all I could afford.
How did you move on from the future we lost,
The love you got and the promise to knot,
If I'm still here trying to experience happiness again,
When I'm not sure what is left more to lose or gain.
How do you sleep knowing I shed my tears for you,
That I promised to stay true and every day I love you anew,
When all I can do is living the past and dream of tomorrow,
Trying hard not to drown in my own sorrow.
How would the past-you react to this new year,
Knowing that it will create fear in the ones dear,
If only you knew how much I try today too,
To keep you happy through everything you go through.
How can I know if all that happened was real,
Or, for you, if it was an unwanted ordeal,
When all I can want is some happiness to borrow,
From the plans, we made for us and our memories of tomorrow.

47. Act of Love

Your heart deserves
To be
Chosen,
Seen,
Understood,
And loved unconditionally.
I hug the pillow
Next to me
Maybe kissed
By your soft skin
So, I can
Finally, wrap your love
Around my heart.
Sometimes hearts are scared
To love too much
When in reality
Regrets come
When you don't love enough.
I look at you
Every time.
I stumble,
Lose balance,
Miss out,
Fall of,

Knees buckle,
Body shivers
But you always bring me
Back onto my feet.
I know
We don't speak often
But I'm still here
When you need me.
If by any chance
You find yourself
Alone again
I will be here always.
The sound of you walking into my life,
Was the softest, sweetest act of love,
That my heart will forever remember.

48. Paradise Love

Your presence is like a forbidden fruit for me, undeniable and sweet.
But ironically too honest to cheat
How can I not fall in love with you?
When your eyes, only search for me in a room full of crowd.
Selfish of me to say but it makes me proud.
You handle my jagged self even though it makes you bleed.
If only I could show you the love I've kept hidden in a void without any
greed.
How can I not fall in love with you?
When you run to me and say
" I've been waiting for you all day long". My name hung on your lips, like
to you it rightfully belong.
But what if I let my guards down and say….
I've never stopped missing you from dusk till dawn.
In this chess of life I'll protect you by being your pawn.
I'll bring you the peace,
By wrapping my arms around you like a fleece.
For the moments I live and die,
Wish I could freeze.
Would you still love me the same?
Now look I've fallen too hard for you
How can I not?
When your mother who fancy me lot,
Is ready to tie us in a knot

If this is a dream then it's too good to be true ,
But when I open my eyes ,
I want myself to be next to you.
Let me stay captivated in your hoaxed paradise.
I'll surrender my heart for you to colonise. If this is a war, the victory is
yours,
My love for you shall forever remain pure.

49. Love is in the Air

I really don't know what love is,
Am I only the one who still miss.
Thinking this made me fall in it,
And I started experiencing it little bit.
Not a normal guy but a cute kiddo,
Not a gym guy but a handsome hero.
Warm welcome when he sees me,
Long talks and his handmade tea.
The way he does stand-up comedy and dance,
God pls make sure I don't miss any chance.
Is he is only the guy who is ruling in my heart,
No way but SM.. I can't leave him apart.
I don't want him but I need his presence,
I don't want relationship but I need his friendship.
Okay, I am in Love and I don't care,
Yes, It's true that Love is in the Air.

50. You And Me

It's a been long journey being with you.

From the day I first saw you and fall in love to the day we hugged for the first time.

From the day you first time spoke to me to the day you first time spoke those three magical words.

With you the whole world feels like a realm ,you are a genius when it comes to understanding what I exactly feel now.

From our first fights to your first cry .

From your fear of lizards to fear of losing me .

We have evolved so much in so less time .

I just want us to stay here take a glimpse of old moments and enjoy the new ones holding our hands together.

In our fights you convince me the best way possible,

when I am down or cranky you cheer me up and show me the hope .

When I am in doubt your shoulders are the best place to find peace .

In the initial stages of life I had a fear of losing you but today all that fear is vanished ,Today I know whatsoever happens iam not letting you go .

I still not believe that when the world felt iam melodramatic,idiotic and foolish you stepped into my life and changed me as a person .

Today the version of mine that the world knows is because of you .

I am happy that I at least have a person to share everything from highs
and lows ,from embarrassments
to proud moments of life .
Please be with me till the end of this book .

51. Story of Love

52. Love Beyond Imagination

My love for you is beyond imagination
It's addiction, attraction
A single moment without you is like decades
My heartbeat skips whenever you are not with me
When I miss you, I think about you
When I think about you, I listen songs
When I do that, I feel that you and me are in act
When I feel that, I become shy
When I become shy, I smile like crazy
When I smile, I hug my teddy
When I do that, I feel that I am huging you
When I feel that, my feeling goes out of this world
When my feeling goes out of this world
I realise how much I love you
When I realise that I love you
Again I miss you so much
Your thoughts sails on my mind wave
Your Love is like low tide
Your arms like shore
Land of love
Covered with grass of care
Flowers bloom as a hope
Mind excites and flew like birds
Colorful dreams of love

Flying in mind like beautiful butterflies
Rain of care, trust, loyalty
Wets your soul
Inhance the beauty of your heart.

53. Propose Day

Every ray of hope I see towards a love
Faded even before I could recognise it;
The tunnel closes into a very sharp end
Making it look like a thorn from outside.
I travel back to my original first raw route
Detoxing feelings, filtering my emotions;
Trying to keep my focus onto destiny,
I walk forward yet at times I take a turn.
Hoping for some unrequited cared love
And also hoping to not get more thorns;
I move forward, the only way visible
The ray piercing through my trackway
You stood there blocking the red rays.
And kept watering when I hesitated,
You held my hurtful past in your hand
Kneeling down on one knee, proposing.
As the rose I blossomed in your care,
Ashamed I felt about my thorn trail;
But you made realize trust and love
Also have been through a rough past.

54. CHOCOLATE DAY

Sun is with brightness in full sway,
Time is flowing in its own way,
Heart is beating with a musical way.
The light of hope is shining in my heart,
Thinking of you,
I am putting chocolate in my cart.
Hoping to see you in the evening
Without expecting myself to be late,
With a red rose in hand and
Coffee with cream and chocolate.
The flavour of my love is very sweet
Just like a Bournville Chocolate,
Hope the sweetness of our love
Will be so caring and loving like milkcake.
Finally, I met you in the evening
You were looking pretty with red skirt and tunic,
You were trying to see my hands with gifts
And like a child you were peeping.
The expression of your face was very kind and sober,
Today, I am grateful that you are my only love and love forever.

55. The Drastic Step

She was desperately breathing for her last few moments,
In the hospital where the nurses demanded a seclusion.
With the oxygen mask on her face which revealed ,
A thousand desires to engage with me.
A strong proposition which every young man bestows,
And a young and beautiful woman longs for.
There it turned the other side down ,
In an impulse the spinster exclaimed in pain.
She was desperate to meet me in a haste ,
As I arranged for a formal proposition on Rose Day .
She pestered her family to lift her in a stretcher ,
To meet her long desired wish and propose her boyfriend.
It seemed a Hindi film shooting in a beautiful garden ,
Where she was escorted by her parents to enthrall her passion.
As she approached the me to reveal her honest feelings,
Tears embellished her eyes with several wails of apprehensions.
She was looking like a pristine flower ,
As if a rose was emanating fragrance in a shower.
My attention directly fell on the girl ,
As she proposed me with a drastic step at large.
Never heard before that a girl proposing a boy,
It was a scene which turned my life upside down in an overjoy.
She passed away in a sensational moment ,
After proposing me she expressed her trust and dependence.

I stood speechless over this tragedy ,
As my beloved was brave in proposing me in such an extremity.
To recall those moments of deep sensitivity ,
I reminiscence the courage of my girlfriend ;
For such a divine proposition in an ephiphany.
I was thereafter married to another maiden whom I met in a tram,
I still couldn't forget any moment of that sensational proposal .
Today I'm a grandfather of four grandchildren ,
As they enjoy the real story of a special moment.
Enthralling over this drastic step ahead,
She will be always enlivening my spirits.

56. The One Life !

Life is something which is always on earth,
They say it is nil when the time comes,
But I experienced the life after that time,
Saw the unbelievable creatures lurking,
Felt their seraphic presence out of my body,
But heard a cry of my heir an infant of mine,
The creatures saw me with filled eye-water,
They grabbed me by elbows & jeered on me,
She's the god's child from the god's heaven,
Its you who have to nurture her and care of,
I was pushed with thousands of gusts,
Just into my open mouth and woken from death,
The infant shown me the utter meaning of life,
Its not a person who come to the being on own,
But a one is born as the continuation of family,
The life is just a meaningless book without the pages of relatives and
sibling
Not all are gifted with the same only chosen one gets that fortune,
So live your and their life !

57. A Dignity To Unite In One Expression In Love

Over an expression of uniting souls in a thread ,
Love knows no religion or language in a perfervid desire to discriminate.
In an assemblage of cherishing a relationship to a divine pleasure ,
Love means respect and sacrifice for each other.
To anyone who seeks an extension of help or compassion,
With benevolence love brings beautiful souls close together.
To understand each other and feel the comfort in an impassion,
The intensity of love raises an attraction in an immersion.
A strong and bold expression to enliven the spirits,
The language of love is one that integrates emotions in a divinity.
Whenever the bells ring to cradle and embolden the spirits,
With an embrace the songs of the Nightingale emboss a melody to cherish.
How credulous it is to embrace in a strong union !
When the care and concern of the worldly affairs;
Would never deter us from making a stringent decision.
To stay forever united in a spheric relation ,
To enjoy a togetherness to enchant in an exhilaration.
To reciprocate the inner feelings without any rest,
To be at each others embrace and forget the world.
In a close proximity when the situations are adverse,
A strong determination always enhances the power of love.
Withdrawing easily from the concurrent situations ,

Is never an intention of the love birds to demotivate in a relation.
To fly high with aspirations and synergy,
Love teaches how best to serve humanity.
To be compassionate to the weak and the destitute ,
To be honest to ones work goals and devotion towards the nation.
To love one's motherland is a blessing altogether,
To worship our parents in an endeavour.
To cradle the child in a forgetfulness,
To sacrifice lives as a martyr in a sensational faithfulness.
To cherish nature at its best,
Or to integrate a nation in unity in diversity concept.
Love follows no barriers of languages or culture,
Its an emotion of beatific relations.
A pleasure that entwines eternal bond ,
A solace of an union where worshipping the relation;
With respect, admiration and care is a possessed treasure.

58. The Burning Desire

The human heart, a curious thing,
With tendencies that take to flight,
From joy and love to greed and spite,
A moon that waxes, wanes, and swings.
The stars that twinkle up above,
A guiding light for all to see,
Yet in our hearts, a fire burns,
A desire that cannot be moved.
We see the world with curious eyes,
And in our minds, the thoughts reveal,
The ones that stir and make us feel,
And show us what is truly real.
A man with fire in his heart,
A flame that burns with all its might,
Exposes what was hidden in plain sight,
And lights a path that sets him apart.
So let us embrace our human traits,
And in the moon and stars find peace,
For though they may wax and wane with ease,
Our burning desires shall not.

59. Month of Love

It's 4 AM, and I want to be in love.
I want to have someone that I can call mine.
I hate being lonely.
But it's all I've known for so long.
I realize now that I just miss the feeling of love,
Not the love itself.
Love is beautiful.
And I want to experience that.
I want to be seen as beautiful in someone's eyes,
I want to see someone, anyone,
As beautiful as love itself.
It's almost valentine's day,
And I'm alone,
And it's so unfortunate.
I don't have to be lonely.
There are people who like me,
But I don't love them,
So, I don't want to be theirs.
I want to fall in love.
I want to know that somebody is there for me,
Cherishing me,
Holding me,
Telling me that I can make it,
Loving me,

Loving me,
Loving me.

60. Love Is So Beautiful

I want a piece of it.
If somebody could love me,
If I could love them back,
It would be so beautiful.
I dream about love.
I feel like I'm living in a loveless world,
I don't crush on people anymore,
And it hurts.
I feel loveless.
But love is so beautiful.
If I could have him,
Everything would be beautiful.
But the world is cruel.
There are so many things that separate us.
I'm so juvenile to even entertain the thought of loving him.
I used to fall in love so easily,
But now, it's like love has been stolen from me.
I don't know when,
Or why, it happened,
But, over the years,
I've just stopped loving.
Maybe, it's because I've stopped loving being alive.
Maybe, it's because I never learned to love myself.
Maybe, it's because I always gave so much,

But, rarely ever got anything in return.
This isn't about anybody.
Don't make it out to be that way.
This is about love.
Love is no person,
No gender,
No race,
No language,
No color,
No creed,
Nothing.
Love is beautiful.
It's 5 AM, and I want to be in love.

61. A Rose With Their Thorns

There is a greatness in rose
Full of positivity
I was walking in my garden and saw the roses are blooming everywhere
Exquisite with red, yellow, white
I see their thorns are guarded them
To blooming happily without any interference
To feel the scent of fragrance
Can't entry without their thorn's permission
Guided themselves to purity within
Roses in thorns is a beauty often
There is nothing without the thorns
Beauty is there with the thorns
Ties a sacred thread of blessing.

62. l'éternité en amour

You brought something in my life,

Which is warm, tender and devoted.

As our tales travelled- certain entities got displaced,

For some where at good and some at the worst.

The dreaming tales were not enacted,

The fairytale love has turned not be our stuff.

We lost all the bits and pieces one after the other,

We ran a marathon of feelings to hold each other.

Held each other inspite of the mishappenings,

But those external interference made it arduous.

They played their hands inculcating hatred inside us,

But still couldn't cumulate the necessaries for hating each other.

The hands that held me when I slumped upon my mishaps,

Couldn't be left all alone to suffer the adversities.

Our love can fix the broken pieces of our stories,

To a whole new amorous escapade.

Our love turned to be painful and downcast for a while,

But it's worth for our bonding for the rest of our lifes.

Amant, Let's get lost in our melancholy souls,

For your solicitude always shows the way back to finding each other.

Even though a lot happen between us but still you owe my heart,

You owe my heart always and forever.

This idea is hard to convince

But you ushered something ravishing which I don't want to loose.

63. One True Love Of Life

Love is a strange word ,
True for some and an illusion to others ,
In end the world is itself an illusion ,
The people here are always two faced ,
Something else in front of someone ,
And a complaint register to others ,
But in my opinion true love exists ,
The one who cares for you at all times ,
Present when happy to celebrate it ,
Whenever devastated there to console you ,
A true friend whom one can trust truly ,
Never regret trusting that someone,
As you would have chosen the best in the world ,
If not continue then search till you find someone ,
The person who accepts you with all flaws ,
Finds the best in you always ,
That one person in life can be your love forever ,
Who holds your hands in darkness ,
Brings you towards the bright side of life ,
Doesn't demand anything but love and respect for each other ,
Let us make our life colorful with love ,
Experience the true love in life with our hearts full.

64. My Voice Will Reach Out To The World

When the depravity and atrocities oppress the women ,
And I am inflicted with a social discrimination ;
My voice will reach out to the world.
To reprimand the evils and the injustices over my existance ,
The regular harassments and humiliations that I bore;
The egregagious behaviours which compel me to rebel,
Must be girded for a combat soon.
When the helplessness and emotional terminations ,
Lead to misery, loneliness and aggressions.
There the voice of a victim, Must rise against the grandiloquent and
malicious minds.
Those forlorn moments of my youth that I recall ,
Resonate each moment whenever;
The reminiscences agonize my soul.
Those excruciating pain which torn my heart apart ,
That seclusion where I was desperate to free my desires.
No one comforted my spirit ,
No one heard my yowl and lamented.
Insecurities gripped my soul, And enforced me into severe depressions.
The trauma exasperated and infuriated my mind ,
Impulsive reactions compelled me to battle this ferocity with my might.
I knew my voice will reach out to the world ,

I knew the pen is mightier than a sword.
My indignant feelings in a vehement cantankerous impulse,
Unbosomed in my expressions through my promulgated poems.
Affected with encumber my bold personality rebelled,
With my weapon (pen) I refuted the injustices;
Which afflicted like an inundation.
That I'm a woman of substance,
That my existence demands respect ;
And recognitions to receive a justice.

65. The Sinking Heart

The teenage love and attractions ,
Those three magical words ,
The rising heart beat ,
The nervousness and shaking of body ,
Those moments that define you being in love ,
This mesmerising event that changes ,
Something eternally forever ,
The body responds to their presence,
Very differently and positively,
But the feeling to be distant ,
Not able to relate or connect,
Then the heart sinks ,
Begging for being recognised,
Those moments that separates you ,
From someone whom you love wholeheartedly,
The atmosphere saddens and lowers itself,
The life freezes for that moment ,
Allowing us to adapt the change ,
Making rejection or that ignorance a part ,
Consoling in its own way ,
The life responds ,
But still the heart sinks ,
The love can't disappear in seconds,
After all teenage is tough ,

Emotions erupt and bust within ,
Still the heart sinks ,
Not accepting the truth ,
Urge to again be in love ,
That is what teens is about ,
Love and heart breaks ,
Making it a remembrance forever ,
For now the heart is broken ,
Sinking with every moment lived .

66. Rose Day/ Roses

And I'm writing this letter to a person, who I admire the most,

With rose tucked inside the cover, so that to doesn't get lost,

She is my life, she is my everything and I will love her the most,

I'm proud of my Mother, and from the borders I'm sending this post.

This photograph is for my world, who stood with me always,

My wife, my beautiful lady, she made me strong and the best,

She was bold enough to help, when I entrusted her for war,

A soldier in me was sad, for he would miss the Rose Day from far.

And this pendant is for the fairy, an angel who makes me proud,

My beautiful daughter smiling, makes my heart smile loud,

Tears are literally nothing, love for her makes my heartbeat,

I've been missing her charming beauty, it's so lonely under the heat.

So, this Rose Day I'm claiming, gifting 'roses' of my heart,

Presenting my life to them, that I miss them as a broken part,

There's a frame I have created, of a happy family living,

Oh! This soldier here is teary eyes, as he promises to keep smiling.

67. I Was Aborted

Abandoned and betrayed
Forsaken and deserted,
Despite your warm companion,
My heart within me like a stone.
Your words each time brought grief to me,
You want me gone,
I wished I could change your mind,
With each tender squeezing, you felt,
I wished you could hear me say,
"We would be fine".
I wished you were not unfaithful
I wished you were not untrue.
Father thought of me as a thorn,
A shame and costly mistake.
The Fruit he was not prepared for.
Father smiled with no grief,
When my demise was told.
If he was given a chance to live,
Why not I?
My hope faded when the pill you took,
And slowly my heart closed its doors.
I was thrown away like a complete waste,
For an unwanted fetus, I was
That wasn't my mistake.

I was ABORTED!
I was a valuable life yearning to live.

• 87 •

68. Loving The Month Of Love

February, a month of love, so sweet and so fine
A time when hearts are filled, with feelings that shine
The chill of winter, is warmed by the fire
Of passion and romance, a love's true desire
The world is a canvas, painted in hues of red
With the colors of love, filling every bed
From roses to chocolates, to poems of rhyme
February spreads love, in its own sweet time
The month of February, is a time of new starts
A time to rekindle, love that was once apart
It's a time to show love, in every little way
From gifts to gestures, that brighten up each day
The snow may be falling, and the winds may be cold
But love warms the heart, and gives love a hold
It's a time to hold hands, and dance in the snow
And celebrate love, that continues to grow
The month of February, is a time of dreams
A time to believe, in the power of love beams
It's a time to wish, for love that endures
And to thank the one, who our love secures
February, a month of love, so warm and so bright
A time to cherish, love that shines so light

So let us celebrate, this month of love's power
And bask in its glow, hour after hour.

• 89 •

So let us celebrate, this month of love's power
And bask in its glow, hour after hour.

69. Rose Day

It's turning 12:00 in the midnight,
You wanna sleep or still continue the fight ?
I asked him when he was leaving home,
Silence and peace left so I thought now he will rome.
Crying eyes gives deep sleep,
Let this love be temporary as everyone is cheap.
At morning 5:00 I heard something interesting,
It seems like birds are piercing and stars are twinkling.
Good morning sweetheart,
Take this beautiful roses and promise, we will never be apart.
As I removed the sheet from face,
He was on his kness and I was totally obsessed.
As I stepped towards him,
Romantic songs played around, am I watching some film ?
North, east, west , south,
I was just hearing "Happy Rose Day Queen" from his mouth.
We did dance and fun together,
And promised each other to stay forever.
What more can I expect from love,
He hasn't slept the whole night and kept his efforts above.
If my Rose day was this much special,
Then Valentine day will be super special.

70. How True Is Your Love

In a generation where the teens can kill for love,
Do you think this passion is enough?
I mean, do you even realise what it means to love with passion?
It isn't something to show off, it needs compassion.
True love is realising that your lover can leave,
True love is in giving with no expectations to receive;
True love is knowing that your lovers' futures matter,
True love is holding on, in sunny or stormy weather.
Because in true love, happiness is in seeing them smile,
In true love, you want to see them in places worthwhile;
True love is loving them for whatever they are,
True love is about caring for them, be it near or far.
But what we call love are mere hollow claims,
So volatile and fragile, it inevitably goes up in flames;
True love is something we barely acknowledge or know,
True love bears no fear in letting them go!
So when you meet your lover, be sure to realise,
They see a shared dream when they look into our eyes;
So next time you hug them, be sure to let them know,
That their dreams do matter, and that together you shall grow !

71. My Love: You are exceptional

You are the most phenomenal person I met,
You are a good-looking man with a golden heart,
I see your authentic colours every day,
You are truthful in your ways,
Don't listen to what others think about you,
Don't try to change yourself into the one you are not,
Yes, your change will pause my heart,
I am sinking in devotion to this man,
I see and know who you are,
I Love the original one with lone spirit and golden heart,
You are the Angel always spreading wings to allow my heart and soul to
rest in your quest,
Your sparkling eyes and comprehensive smile,
It fills me with joy and pride,
This tiny beard and shiny glimmer,
Holding a surprise every time,
Your presence makes happiness so deep,
I confess "I Love You", my love for being who you are,
You are exceptional with excellence at par,
Your connection is deep and reaching the soul,
I feel it's a miracle from far,
I pay gratitude to the universe for

Allowing me to grace you with the darling you are,
I will walk the dusk with you to the Enternity and beyond far.

• 93 •

72. Love

Love is a word which is used by many,
For some it is an emotion but for some it is penny.
Going to the olden times, love was a beauty,
Now a days, who puts their heart out truly?
The feeling of love is just mesmerizing,
Each and every moment which you spend together is surprising!
Being there for each other when the situations are broke,
You have to believe in each other rest all should be all smoke.
The stages of love are like stepping stones,
Climbing through difficulties to reach the love thrones.
It is all about you staying there and not leaving at the situation,
All you have to do is go deeper in the love meditation.

73. Primrose

The sun seems a shade darker
A crimson anger, bubbles from its core
Has the damage made by us, forced him to change,
The mighty and forgiving primrose?
The moon seems so far away
No northern star shows the light,
The ocean looks like an inky sea
With no starry reflection to adorn the sight.
Men are dying on the streets
Disguised sinners roam out free,
Is this the end, the wise men predicted
The troubled death of you and me?
An apology won't be accepted
For it seems the water is over the brink
And if we die, let it be together,
Let us hold hands while we sink.
But before that, let us bow
And ask for forgiveness, on our knees
The nature we killed, the rivers we dried
Apologize to the Gods of the heavenly seas.
Let us ask for mercy from the universe
The primrose, stars, and the moon
And ask to be reborn, with a conscious mind
To never cause destruction and doom.

74. Remember the Roses

Glorified as a sign of love , compassion and eternal beauty ,
Rose is the queen of flowers which is beautiful, appealing and attractive.
So divine is its fragrance ,
That everyone is in an oblivion to witness its elegance.
Roses enchant and enthrall us in different shapes , sizes , colours and
patterns ,
White , yellow , pink and red rejuvinate us with a fragrance, That seems
to calm us in a gentility and
warmth.
When the mind indulges in a winsome and wacky , turmoil,
The beautiful flower always instill a motivation and vigour.
Unfolding the pages of a chapter in a book,
Often a reminiscence of the past uplifts the spirits;
While holding the torn petals of this flower.
Keeping it inside the book as a fond memory ,
Gives a divine touch to that person's gift in an endeavor to treasure so
unabashed.
That unbroken heart searches for the love which perhaps enlivens ,
Those glorious moments when the lovers spent together in a close
proximity.
The tiny thorns pricks at times to remind,
Life is not a bed of roses that we can;
Always hope for the best to embrace and abide.

Grown in shrubs they spread the fragrance,
Perhaps Cupid throws an arrow on the buds from above ;
And rejoices over the garlands that the wreaths are adorned.
To the newly weds or the lovers on Valentine's day,
To uplift passion and sensation to cheer up the melancholic situation.
As W.B. Yeats fondly related that like a casket of gold,
This beautiful flower blossomed in his dreams in memory of his beloved
lover.
Whispering to the beautitude of nature ,
White roses symbolises peace ,
Yellow roses symbolises friendship and pink roses symbolises gratefulness
and joy.
The delicate petals attract a beholder ,
Who smells it over and over again.
A purity that it relates to the whole world,
Would continue to cheer several celebrations and gatherings for more
fervour.

75. Roses

A small symbol of love
A small gift to show my gratitude
Really thankful of God
For sending the biggest blessing of my life as you
A Rose for someone who is prettier than the flower..
It is the perfect symbol, which represents how perfect you are..
Not sure how this small flower became the symbol of love for the world..
But let me tell you how this rose is the perfect representation of my world..
Maybe not the rarest one , but the one which clearly stands out ..
Hundreds of others flowers are there, but none as beautiful as you..
Your smile is like it's fragrance, enough to soothe my heart..
Your generosity similar to its beauty, which sets you apart..
The blush on your face while reading these lines, making it bright red..
Tell me my little rose, how any other flower can even compare ..
Your innocence making you as delicate as it's petals are..
Your intelligence and stubbornness are the thorns,
For those who want to hurt you , keeping them far..
Let me gift the rose of love to the prettiest rose out here..
Maybe too common for others ,but on seeing your smile ,I don't really
care..

76. The Rose Of Love

A sad morning,

Struggling with mixed emotions!!

Suddenly my mind says,

Go for it..

And I am ready to commit a suicide!!

Must be thinking,

Why??

Yes,a big story and a big cheating..

Someone dumped me..

Because my complexion is dark..

Suddenly when I am in my balcony my heart says hey dear,you "My

darling baby,I am proud of you..

doesn't matter what someone say about u understood..

This words are my strength for life says by my papa!!..

He says this word on rose day by gifting a red rose to me..!!

77. Flowering Hope

Leaves fading away,
Roots weakening,
Body pulling me away,
My mind whimpering ..
Let my Heart be Brave!
Stormy weather,
Gusty windows,
Thundering makes all stem naked,
Flowers closing up,
Knowing their end is approaching.
Life is at a pause.

78. Let My Heart stay Calm !

Welcome Twists and turns,
However at the end of the day,
It's Me who yearns,
As everyone is on their way to betray!
Let Gladiolus give me Hope,
Let Cosmos bless me with peace,
Let Chamomile flowers relieve my stress,
Let Orange Blossom love me,
Let the Iris flower hold my hand in the darkest hour,
Cherishing me as a best friend.
Let my Heart have a new beginning with Golden Daffodils.
New petals, new buds
New Life, new hope
Is all being planted
In my Garden of Hope .

79. Where are you?

Sometimes I just run…
Find a place to hide.
My world comes crashing down
And I just wanna die.
Sometimes I just wanna crawl,
Underneath my bed.
The voices get so loud,
Deep inside my head.
The pain is so intense,
I just wanna cry.
What's wrong with me…
Someone tell me why.
It's getting kinda late,
It's the middle of the night.
I know you're upset,
But l don't wanna fight.
Why don't you understand,
Why can't I make you see?
You're the one who said
You'd always stand by me.
Hold me thru the night,
Take away my pain.
Your love the thing that
Keeps me from going insane.

Babe, I'm so scared,
It's getting hard to breathe.
I know you're upset,
But please don't leave.

80. Loving You

Today a drummer boy told me you are falling in love with me
Or was it your heart beating when I kissed the bosom of thee
It was the time when the Nox was at her young
And I was kissing you and its silence who sung
In the midst of the dark
I held you tight in Hyde's park
You were truly looking something
Like an angel spreading her wing
I felt it is not the beauty for which I should love you
It is not the quality at all for what I must trust you
But is thou's way of giving love
And the way you want to be loved
Whilst I kissed you from top to toes
Your soft body felt like a winter rose
Oh so soft, as one can be
Softness that was never earlier felt by me
I drank wine every time I kissed your lips
You tried to speak but they only lisp
I wished from heart to keep loving you
Till the sun shower snow & eternity will be new.

81. Hopelessly In Love

Before I met you,
I felt that I couldn't love anyone,
That nobody would be able to fill the void in my heart,
But that all changed when I met you.
Then I came to realize you were always on my mind.
You're funny and sweet.
You make me laugh and smile.
You take away all my anger and sadness.
You make me weak when I talk to you.
Then I started to write poems about you.
Now I have come to realize that I am hopelessly in love with you.

82. Love Sits On my Shoulder

Love sits on my shoulder and whispers in my ear.
It tells me how you love me and the words I want to hear.
Love is growing with you and filling in the gaps.
Love is our tomorrows, our future, and our past.
Love binds the ties together and secures them with a knot.
Love is our plans that we outgrew and the ones that we forgot.
Love is what we've had together, all these blessed years.
Love sits on my shoulder and whispers in my ear.

83. Loving Moments

I have a feeling
That I can't comprehend.
In my deepest thoughts you are
More than just a friend.
I wouldn't want to
Rush us now
As love we explore,
But there's a growing love inside
That we just can't ignore.
I love the times we
Spend together. We are comfortable
And free. I think of you when we are
Alone. I think of you and me.
We have shared
Secrets to uncover. There's more
To life. We will both discover.
I love you always.
I'll love you when you're dumb,
I'll love you when you're smart,
I'll love you any way you are,
Right from the start.
I'll love you if you're tall
I'll love you if you're short,
I'll love you if you're pretty,

Or just an ugly dork.
I'll love you if you're toothless,
I'll love you if you're blind,
Anything that's wrong with you,
To me you'll be fine.
My heart is opening up now,
Unlike it used to do.
I see the pain that's in your heart,
And sometimes I feel it too.
I'll love you tomorrow,
I'll love you today,
I'll love you forever,
And forever always.

84. Love Of Your Eyes

When I am looking into your eyes,
I see all the love you have for me.
I see in your eyes you care for me a lot.
I see your love for me is true,
And you will do whatever it takes to have me in your life.
When I am looking into your eyes,
I see your love for me is unconditional.
Your eyes tell me you will never leave me.
You will always stay by my side
To protect and cherish me.
When I am looking into your eyes,
I see with you everything is possible.
I see in your eyes your love for me is everlasting.
Your eyes tell me you really, really love me.

85. The Real Meaning Of Love

To love is to share life together,
To build special plans just for two,
To work side by side,
And then smile with pride,
As one by one, dreams all come true.
To love is to help and encourage
With smiles and sincere words of praise,
To take time to share,
To listen and care
In tender, affectionate ways.
To love is to have someone special,
One on whom you can always depend
To be there through the years,
Sharing laughter and tears,
As a partner, a lover, a friend.
To love is to make special memories
Of moments you love to recall,
Of all the good things
That sharing life brings.
Love is the greatest of all.
I've learned the full meaning
Of sharing and caring

And having my dreams all come true;
I've learned the full meaning
Of being in love
By being and loving with you.

86. First Official Date

You sat with me under the shade of the trees,
Reading out the words that made no sense,
Not once did you lose faith,
Or let me be,
The slow and steady learner,
The butt of all the jokes,
Duffer! Failure! And more…
Echo's of laughter filling the silence,
As truly we enjoyed each other,
Your lame jokes also I appreciated,
As you teased me for being picky.
Unknowingly our hands brush each other's,
A wave of sensation passing through.
You hold me tight and pulled me in your arms,
Our lips colliding with each other,
A day so normal suddenly became special,
As we enjoyed truly….

87. First Meeting

I had poured my love writing poetries,
Stories of love as we lived so long,
You are my charm, I can fully agree,
You are my sweet melodious song…
You are tune of my heart,
I love you forever, forever…

88. Chocolate – Love Of Many

Chocolate is very tasty to eat and it tastes really sweet, there is no other dessert like Chocolate, and it is
the love of many.
A chocolate can also be gifted to the one whom you love, it's the favorite of many, it's the love of many,
from children to adult everyone eat chocolate, and the smell of it is so pleasant.
Chocolate given by someone hold so much of memories, and we eat the Chocolate and keep the cover
in rememberence of that time and the person whom have give it.
A chocolate looks so dark, tastes so sweet and it smell's really bright, some wish to have a chocolate
world and its some dreams of childhood days. Chocolate, brownies and lava cake is really good to taste.
Chocolate is used for many purpose and it's the love of many. If your loved one is angry you can give
them a chocolate with love just to make them happy,
Chocolate will bring a smile on the face and it will create sweetness in your bond.
" CHOCOLATE IS A DESSERT WHICH YOU YOU HAPPINESS WHENEVER IT MELT ON YOUR TONGUE"

89. Melting Hearts With Chocolate

Joys of surprise and amazement must astonish ,
The creatures dwelling in the forest in a bliss.
When the rain pours in a susurous rapture ,
That fills the ponds and streams;
With chocolates in an eclectic feeling.
The humans enjoy this taste in a celebration ,
Why it is not arranged for the animals in a derivation ?
With drum beats as the party begins ,
The zebra , giraffe , kangaroos and deer grins.
With wide open arms as the orangutans cheer ,
The lions and the cheetah 's will endear.
That moment of ecstasy in an union ,
That chocolate river brings innumerable happiness ;
And divine spirit in a festive fervour.
Chocolates instill joy and exhilaration ,
The tastes are heavenly like a nectar .
When in melancholy or in stress ,
Chocolates raise a good spirit to smile and relate.
How beatitude pervades a situation ,
When the cocoa is mixed with ingredients in a treasure.
That holy enigma acclaims a veracious attempt and verb.

90. Chocolate

Chocolate is yummy and everyone what's to eat them.

Be it a Chocolate bar ,a wafer, toffee or just a pack of gems.

Chocolate can bring people together and make them friends forever.

Chocolate is a sweet ,which when eaten makes you wiser and clever.

Chocolate can be eaten for breakfast, lunch or at anytime.

But giving someone whom you admire ,a Chocolate is not a crime.

No one can really resist a Chocolate, can eat it in a car or just home.

Some will want to share their precious Chocolate or just go out to roam.

Chocolate is a sweet which will just melt down on your tongue.

And will make you say aloud to all around you ,oh! That was a pleasing one.

When you want to be friends with someone the first thing we prefer to share is a Chocolate.

Yes ,my dear friends there is nothing that is more sweeter and appealing than a Chocolate.

91. Chocolaty Moments

Hey, what says the chocolates
These are really delicious pockets
Sweet, creamy & milky is our relation prime
*She got *KITKAT* which means*
Kiss In Time, Kiss At Time
Our love is full of mug
*She gives me *MUNCH* which means*
Meet Urgently Now for a Charming Hug
We love each other & we miss
*We share our *PERK* which means*
Perfect Emotional Romantic Kiss
Hey, what says the chocolates
These are really delicious pockets…
Will You Watch The Sky With Me
Will you hold my hand,
Walking on the sand.
Will you adore my smile,
On a busy day, working while.
Will you watch the moon with me,
Till the love inside us flow free.
Will you stand by my side,
When the world leaves me aside.
Will you see the pain hidden
In my eyes,

When the world is unable to realise.
Will you be my sunshine,
Till the world starts to decline,
World starts to decline.

92. The Melting Heart

The heart felt mushy when you came ,
It melted like a chocolate,
The purity of white chocolate,
And bitterness of dark chocolate,
In the month of February,
The valentine week that celebrated love ,
Had that purity and bitterness of chocolate,
That on chocolate day for every lover ,
Not only them but a friendship needs occasional refreshment,
Like any day chocolate was given with love ,
Thanking many for being there ,
Or appreciating the fact that no one is perfect ,
And accepting one another,
May the most of every bitterness in life is handled with the purity,
That gave away the sweetness entirely ,
For every person to cherish and celebrate,
Not only on a day each year but for the life ,
Wishing chocolate day to every lover and friends,
And praying that this sweetness would sweeten the trust for each other ,
And let you continue engaging yourself in care ,
And the possessiveness for loved ones ,
Let the chocolate define you in and out for better .

93. Bonding Between Two Lovers

Dark goes when the light comes,
Hate disappears when love appears;
Time may tie us with a busy schedule,
The season may chase us one after,
But we are united together,
As we are bind with true souls;
The bond is tested with the fate:
Fate brings up the duel,
When clashes arouse within us
There is no need to rise a rose,
Because love doesn't expect anything ;
It is an unconditional one between us.
Our direction may be differ;
But our destination is success;
In the same way, my destiny is to conquer your heart
I am alive to write this poem because of you my dear.
In my life, you are a priceless gift.

94. True Love

Love is not something readymade.
Its reached to you with someone who,
Cares for you ,respect you and love you in every prase of life.
Love gives us the freedom to live the life
How we want to live.
Love is beautiful feeling of being special for someone.
Love don't have any boundaries.
Love gives us wings to fly openly.
Love is pure feeling .
Love is like friendship.
It can be with your parents, your relatives,
Someone special one.
Love is the biggest positive feeling.
Love is multicolour happiness.
Love is everything, its have happiness, respect, peace, interest, hope, pride,
honour, motivation, believe,
trust, joy.
Love is when two people's touch each one soul and its feeling of connection
of two hearts.
True love stories never have endings.
True love become stronger with time.
True love never deals with any condition.
Love is key to open the doors of happiness.
Love is when someone touching your soul.

Love is something where you shares your secret in the company.
You enjoy the company of your loved once.
Real love never ends, it's last forever.
Every moment you feel lovely.

95. Teddy Bear Is More Than A Friend

Teddy bear, Teddy bear,
You are my forever favorite,
I can talk with you like,
A real best friend of mine.
Teddy bear with very pretty in pink and red colour,
It is so wonderful to see,
The fur of it feels so good,
It is very soft to touch.
Teddy bear is kept,
With a great care,
More like a small baby,
Sleeping on the bedroom.
Teddy bear is a special gift,
That can be given to special one,
Teddy bear can make them remember,
The way you love them.
Sometimes we can share,
All the feelings to teddy bear,
If you lonely your teddy will always be there,
And you can hug your teddy bear,
Whenever you need.

Teddy bear can be our best friend,
Teddy bear will be a best companion,
Because no one stay forever,
But teddy bear Will always there.
Teddy bear is my favorite toy,
I can play with it anytime, At the same time it's my friend,
Who always be there.
I REALLY LOVE MY TEDDY BEAR
HAPPY TEDDY DAY

96. Roses

Roses are red, violets are blue,
On this special day, I think of you.
With each passing moment, my love grows,
Every moment with you, my heart overflows.
You light up my world, with your beautiful smile,
With you by my side, life seems so worthwhile.
In your arms, I find my true home,
Together we'll face the world, hand in hand we'll roam.
So on this day of love, I give you my heart,
With you, my life is a beautiful work of art.
Forever and always, I'll be by your side,
Together we'll make our love, grow with each passing tide.
Happy Valentine's Day, my love, my heart, my all,
With you, I'm whole, I stand tall.
I love you now and forever more,
Forever and always, you're the one I adore.

97. Valentine's Day

On this day of love and cheer,
I want to show how much I hold you dear.
With a heart that beats just for you,
I whisper softly, my love is true.
In your arms, I find my home,
Where I feel safe, and never alone.
Together we walk hand in hand,
Building memories we'll always understand.
With every kiss and every hug,
I promise to love you, more than a bug.
I'll be there in the good and the bad,
With a love that's strong and never fades.
So on this Valentine's Day, I pray,
That our love will forever stay.
And with each sunrise and every sunset,
My love for you will never forget.

98. Love Being So Grateful

My heart beats fast with every thought of you,
With every moment, I feel it grow.
You are the light that brightens up my day,
The one who brings me happiness in every way.
You fill my life with laughter, joy and love,
And I'm so grateful for the blessings from above.
Your smile, your touch, your gentle embrace,
Brings comfort to me in every place.
I'm blessed to have you in my life,
And I want to spend the rest of it as your wife.
So on this Valentine's Day, I want to say,
That I love you more and more each day.
Forever and always, my heart belongs to you,
And I'll love you until the skies turn blue.
Happy Valentine's Day, my love, I pray,
That we'll be together always, come what may.

99. My love

My love for you is like a rose,

Its beauty never fades away.

It grows and blooms with each new day,

And fills my life with its sweet aroma.

You are the sun that lights my life,

The one who makes my heart skip a beat.

Your smile, your laughter, your touch so sweet,

All these things and more make you my wife.

With each passing moment, I feel

The depth of my love for you grow stronger.

I promise to love you now and forever,

And cherish every moment we spend together.

So here's to us, my love,

To a love that will forever thrive.

I give you my heart, my soul, my life,

Together, forever, always by your side.

100. Your Eyes

Your eyes, a deep brown hue
Reflect a warmth that shines through
Your smile, a gentle curve
It lights up my world, that's for sure
The sound of your laughter, like music to my ear
Makes every worry disappear
Your touch, a comfort like no other
It's a love that will last forever
In your arms, I feel safe and secure
No matter the distance, I know you'll endure
Your love, a true gift from above
It's the reason I wake up to love
So here I am, confessing my heart
It beats only for you, it's a work of art
I promise to cherish, to hold and to love
Forever and always, you're my dove.

101. My Reflections: A Journey Through Life

My heart beats fast with excitement,
My thoughts race with anticipation.
My soul sings with joy and delight,
My spirit soars with pure elation.
My mind is filled with creativity,
My imagination runs wild and free.
My hands can craft beauty with ease,
My dreams bring my heart's fantasy.
My eyes take in the world around me,
My ears hear melodies both sweet and low.
My voice echoes with honesty,
My laughter shines like a rainbow.
My journey in life has just begun,
My path ahead is yet unwritten.
My hopes and aspirations are many,
My future is a bright horizon.
My heart aches with love,
My soul soars with passion,
My mind dances with imagination,
My spirit filled with a sense of peace.
My hands shake with excitement,
My feet move with eagerness,

My voice whispers with yearning,
My eyes filled with tears of joy.
My world is a canvas,
My dreams are the colors,
My life a masterpiece,
My destiny an open book.
My journey is long,
My road filled with twists and turns,
My faith is my guide,
My future filled with hope and love.
My journey continues, with each step I take,
My spirit remains strong, no matter what awaits.
My heart remains open, to all that comes my way,
My life is a blessing, each and every day.
My heart aches with sorrow
My soul is filled with pain
My mind races with worry
My eyes can't seem to refrain
My spirit feels broken
My thoughts are far away
My world is shattered
My hope begins to fray
My voice is lost in silence
My path is filled with thorns
My tears fall like rain
My journey feels forlorn.
My dreams are just a memory
My future seems so unclear
My soul is in turmoil

My heart is full of fear
My remembrance will be
My strength and my resolve
My faith in a brighter tomorrow,
My love that I'll always involve.
My mind is a storm, brewing with thoughts and ideas
My eyes are a window, reflecting the world within me
My voice is a bird, soaring with melodies and songs
My spirit is a flame, burning with passion and fire.
My heart is a canvas, painted with love and passion,
My mind is a library, filled with stories of the past and present action,
My soul is a symphony, harmonizing with the beat of life's fashion,
My spirit is a bird, soaring high with limitless satisfaction.
My laughter is a spark, igniting joy in the dullest situation,
My tears are a river, washing away the pain and frustration,
My voice is a breeze, carrying the words of truth and inspiration,
My touch is a flame, warming hearts with comforting elation.
My journey is a road, winding through ups and downs of destination,
My dreams are a lighthouse, guiding me towards my true aspiration,
My passion is a fire, burning bright with purpose and determination,
My love is a rose, blooming with beauty and sweet fragrance sensation.
My heart is a caged bird, singing songs of freedom.
My soul is a ship, sailing on an endless sea of hope.
My mind is a maze, twisting and turning with endless thoughts.
My eyes are a window, revealing all that lies within me.
My voice is a symphony, echoing through the halls of time.
My laughter is a river, flowing with joy and delight.
My tears are a rainstorm, cleansing away the pain and sorrow.
My touch is a flame, burning with passion and intensity.

My spirit is a fire, illuminating the darkness within me.
My heart is a garden, blooming with love and light.
My soul is a river, flowing with peace and might.
My mind is a maze, filled with thoughts and ideas.
My spirit is a bird, soaring high with no fears.
My eyes are the stars, shining bright in the night.
My voice is a song, echoing with delight.
My touch is a spark, igniting passion and fire.
My presence is a breeze, blowing away all the mire.
My love is a rose, blooming with beauty and grace.
My being is a gift, sent from the heavens to bless this place.
My heart is a bird that flutters with delight,
My soul is a river that flows with pure light,
My thoughts are the winds that whisper secrets at night.
My love is a rose that blooms in summer's sun,
My dreams are the stars that dance when day is done,
My life is a song that sings of joy and fun.
My spirit is a flame that burns with endless fire,
My mind is a maze that leads to my desire,
My words are the rain that quenches life's great choir.
My hopes are the clouds that paint the sky with grace,
My fears are the waves that crash upon my face,
My laughter is sunshine that brings a warm embrace.
My memories are the leaves that fall from autumn trees,
My tears are the diamonds that sparkle in the breeze,
My dreams are the butterflies that soar with ease.
My hands are a bridge, connecting me to the world
My feet are roots, grounding me to the earth
My laughter is a sunbeam, spreading joy and light

My tears are a rain shower, cleansing and purifying.